Contents

Welcome to Italy!

Hello! My name is Benjamin Blog and this is Barko Polo, my **inquisitive** dog. (He is named after ancient ace explorer **Marco Polo**.) We have just got back from our latest adventure – exploring Italy. We put this book together from some of the blog posts we wrote on the way.

France

Germany

Slovakia

Switzerland — Liechtenstein

Austria

A L P S

Hungary

Dolomites

Slovenia

Milan

Croatia

Turin

Po Valley

Bosnia-Herzegovina

ITALY

Ligurian Sea

A P E N N I N E S

Adriatic Sea

Rome

Naples

Sardinia

Tyrrhenian Sea

Mediterranean Sea

Sicily

Mount Etna

Ionian Sea

BARKO'S BLOG-TASTIC ITALY FACTS

Italy is a country in Europe. It is shaped like a long, high-heeled boot. Italy has a very long coastline. On land, it is joined to France, Switzerland, Austria and Slovenia in the north.

The story of Italy

Posted by: Ben Blog | 10 September at 2.39 p.m.

The first stop on our tour was the mighty Colosseum in Rome. It was built by the ancient Romans in around AD 70–80. The Romans flocked here to watch **gladiator** fights and wild beast shows – they loved it! It must have been an amazing sight.

BARKO'S BLOG-TASTIC ITALY FACTS
Italy is famous for its artists and painters, and Leonardo da Vinci (1452–1519) was one of the most brilliant. His statue stands outside the Uffizi Art Gallery in Florence.

Volcanoes, mountains, lakes and islands

Posted by: Ben Blog | 28 October at 8.44 a.m.

From Rome, we headed to the island of Sicily, just off the "toe" of Italy. I wanted to climb up Mount Etna. It is the highest volcano in Europe and it is still **active**, so I had to watch my step. If you don't fancy walking, you can take the train that runs around the volcano.

BARKO'S BLOG-TASTIC ITALY FACTS
The Apennines are a mountain range that runs for around 1,400 kilometres (870 miles) right down the middle of Italy. The highest peak is Corno Grande at 2,912 metres (9,554 feet).

Next, we travelled right to the other end of Italy to visit lovely Lake Garda in the north. It is the largest lake in Italy and a great place for a holiday, any time of year. In summer, you can go sailing or windsurfing on the lake. In winter, you can head for the ski slopes nearby.

BARKO'S BLOG-TASTIC ITALY FACTS

Many islands lie around the Italian coast. One of the biggest islands is Sardinia. The Monte Arcosu Oasis is a **nature reserve** there. It is home to more than 1,000 Sardinian red deer.

11

City sights

Posted by: Ben Blog | 22 December at 4.33 p.m.

Today, it was back to Rome, the capital city of Italy. There are hundreds of Roman ruins to see, and lots more besides. This is the Trevi Fountain. Legend says that if you throw a coin in the fountain, you will surely return to Rome one day. Here goes…

BARKO'S BLOG-TASTIC ITALY FACTS

The city of Venice is built on a group of islands in a **lagoon**. The islands are linked by canals, and you have to get about by boat. The Grand Canal is the city's main "street".

Buongiorno!

Most people in Italy speak Italian. *Buongiorno!* means "Good day!" Then you can ask *Come stai?*, which means "How are you?" You can say *Ciao!* to mean "Hello!" or to say "Goodbye!", but only if you know the person (or dog) you are talking to. *Ciao*, Barko!

BARKO'S BLOG-TASTIC ITALY FACTS

Family life is very important to people in Italy. Families like to spend time together. They enjoy meeting up for meals at home or in restaurants, especially at the weekend.

From the ages of 6 to 11, Italian children go to a *scuola elementare* (primary school). From ages 11 to 13, they go to middle school. After this, they have to choose to go to a school that specializes in **academic** subjects, or one that focuses on the arts, technical subjects or languages.

BARKO'S BLOG-TASTIC ITALY FACTS

Many Italians live in or near cities but some live in villages in the countryside. In the centre of the village is the **piazza**, where people go to meet friends and celebrate special occasions.

It's Easter Day and we're back in Rome for a very special event. The Pope is giving his Easter talk to a packed crowd in St Peter's Square, here in Vatican City. The Pope is the head of the **Roman Catholic** Church. Most people in Italy are Roman Catholics.

BARKO'S BLOG-TASTIC ITALY FACTS

Every year, usually in February, a **carnival** takes place in Venice. People dress up in beautiful costumes decorated with gold, crystals and feathers. Their masks are made from leather, clay or glass.

Buon appetito!

Posted by: Ben Blog | 2 May at 5.22 p.m.

After a hard day's sightseeing, we stopped off for something to eat. Italy is famous for yummy pasta and pizza. In a **pizzeria**, the pizzas are baked in a brick oven. I've ordered a margherita pizza, with tomatoes and cheese. I can't wait to tuck in!

BARKO'S BLOG-TASTIC ITALY FACTS

Coffee is a very popular drink in Italy, but you need to know what to order. An espresso is a small cup of strong, black coffee. A cappuccino is a large cup of frothy, milky coffee.

Opera and footbull

Posted by: Ben Blog | 11 June at 11.30 a.m.

Our next stop was the city of Milan. La Scala is probably the most famous **opera** house in the world. We're here to watch an opera. Opera is a type of musical play that began in Italy and spread around the world. Sshhh! The curtain's about to go up...

BARKO'S BLOG-TASTIC ITALY FACTS

Football is the most popular sport in Italy. Italians are football-mad. The national team is called the Azzurri ("light blues") after the colour of its strip. *Forza, Azzurri!* (Go, Azzurri!)

From Chianti to the catwalk

Italy is one of the world's biggest wine-makers. These **vineyards** in Chianti grow grapes for making into wine that is famous around the world. Farmers in the Italian countryside also grow fruit, vegetables, nuts (such as almonds) and olives for making into olive oil.

And finally...

Our trip is nearly over, but I couldn't leave Italy without visiting Pompeii. In AD 79, Mount Vesuvius, a volcano near Naples, erupted and buried the town of Pompeii in ash. People were killed instantly. You can still see the ruins of the town today – it's a ghostly sight.

BARKO'S BLOG-TASTIC ITALY FACTS

Fashion is very important in Italy. Twice a year, there are fashion shows in Milan. Here the fashion houses, such as Gucci and Armani, show off their latest designs.

BARKO'S BLOG-TASTIC ITALY FACTS

The "Leaning Tower" of Pisa started to lean when it was being built in the 12th century. One side sank into the soil. **Engineers** have now made the tower safe, but it is still lopsided.

Italy fact file

Area: 301,336 square kilometres
(116,358 square miles)

Population: 61,680,122 (2014)

Capital city: Rome

Other main cities: Milan, Naples, Turin

Language: Italian

Main religion: Christianity (**Roman Catholic**)

Highest mountain: Monte Bianco de Courmayeur
(4,748 metres/15,577 feet)

Longest river: Po (628 kilometres/405 miles)

Currency: Euro

Italy quiz

Find out how much you know about Italy with our quick quiz.

1. How do you say "Good day" in Italian?
a) *Buon appetito*
b) *Buongiorno*
c) *Forza, Azzurri!*

2. Where is Mount Etna?
a) Sicily
b) Sardinia
c) Naples

3. What is a cappuccino?
a) a type of pizza
b) a type of wine
c) a type of coffee

4. Which city has canals instead of streets?
a) Venice
b) Rome
c) Milan

5. What is this?

Glossary

academic to do with learning and study

active describes a volcano that is still erupting

carnival spectacular festival with music, dancing and fancy dress

engineer person who designs or builds buildings or structures

gladiator Roman fighter

inquisitive interested in learning about the world

lagoon stretch of salt water cut off from the sea by a low sandbank or coral reef

Marco Polo explorer who lived from about 1254 to 1324. He travelled from Italy to China.

nature reserve land set aside for wildlife where it cannot be harmed

opera drama with music, singing and acting

piazza large square in the middle of a town or village

pizzeria restaurant where pizzas are cooked

Roman Catholic Christian who belongs to the Roman Catholic Church

vineyard place where grape vines are grown

Find out more

Books

Italy (Been There), Annabel Savery (Wayland, 2011)

Italy (Countries Around the World), Claire Throp (Raintree, 2012)

Italy (Countries in Our World), Ann Weil (Franklin Watts, 2012)

Italy (Unpacked), Clive Gifford (Wayland, 2013)

Websites

ngkids.co.uk
National Geographic's website has lots of information, photos and maps of countries around the world.

www.worldatlas.com
Packed with information about various countries, this website includes flags, time zones, facts, maps and timelines.

Index